Ukulele

Disney
ENCANTO

Music from the Motion Picture Soundtrack
Original Songs by Lin-Manuel Miranda

ISBN 978-1-70516-365-8

Visit Hal Leonard Online at
www.halleonard.com

Contact us:
Hal Leonard
7777 West Bluemound Road
Milwaukee, WI 53213
Email: info@halleonard.com

In Europe, contact:
Hal Leonard Europe Limited
42 Wigmore Street
Marylebone, London, W1U 2RY
Email: info@halleonardeurope.com

In Australia, contact:
Hal Leonard Australia Pty. Ltd.
4 Lentara Court
Cheltenham, Victoria, 3192 Australia
Email: info@halleonard.com.au

The Family Madrigal

Music and Lyrics by Lin-Manuel Miranda

The home __ of the Fam - ily Mad - ri - gal. __ We're on our way!
The home __ of the Fam - ily Mad - ri - gal! __ Hey, com - ing through!

Where all __ the peo - ple are __ fan-tas - ti - cal __ and mag - i - cal, __
I know __ it sounds __ a bit __ fan-tas - ti - cal __ and mag - i - cal, __ But

1.

I'm part __ of the Fam - ily Mad - ri - gal! __
I'm part __ of the Fam - ily Mad -

2.   **Bridge 1**

- ri - gal! __   Two guys __ fell in love with Fam - ily Mad-

- ri - gal __   And now they're part __ of the Fam - ily Mad-

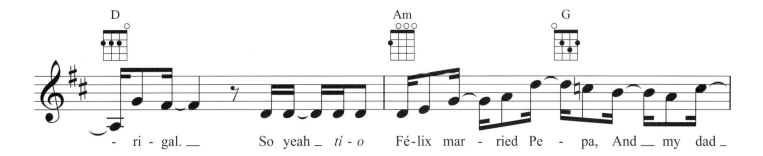

-ri - gal. __ So yeah _ *tí - o* Fé - lix mar - ried Pe - pa, And __ my dad _

___ mar - ried __ Ju - li - e - ta, That's _ how A - bue - la be - came an *A - bue - la* Mad-

Bridge 2

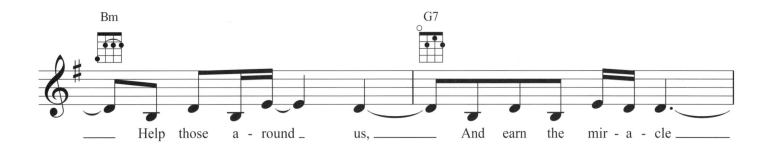

ABUELA ALMA:

- ri - gal! __ Let's go, let's go!   We swear to al - ways __

___ Help those a - round _ us, _____ And earn the mir - a - cle _____

___ That some - how found us.   The town _ keeps _ grow - ing,

The world _ keeps _ turn - ing, But work and __ ded - i - ca - tion ___ Will

keep the mir - a - cle burn - ing. And each new ___ gen - er - a - tion ___ Must

keep the mir - a - cle burn - ing...

Interlude

TOWN KIDS: *Wait— who's a sister and who's a cousin?*

There's so many people! *How do you keep them all straight?*

MIRABEL:

O - kay, o - kay, o - kay, o - kay...

So man - y kids in our house, so let's ___ turn the sound up!

TOWN KIDS & TOWNSPEOPLE:

You know why? __ I think __ it's time __ for a grand - kid round up! Grand - kid round up!

Verse

MIRABEL:

3. Cous - in Do - lor - es can hear a pin ___ drop...

Ca - mi - lo shape ____ shifts, An - to - ni - o gets ___ his gift ___ to - day!

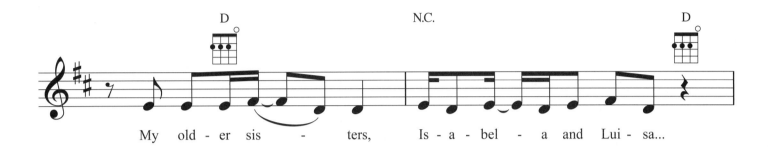

My old - er sis - ters, Is - a - bel - a and Lui - sa...

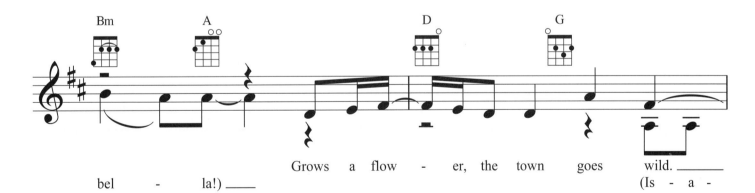

One strong, one grace - ful— Per - fect __ in ev - 'ry way! **TOWNSPEOPLE:** (Is - a -

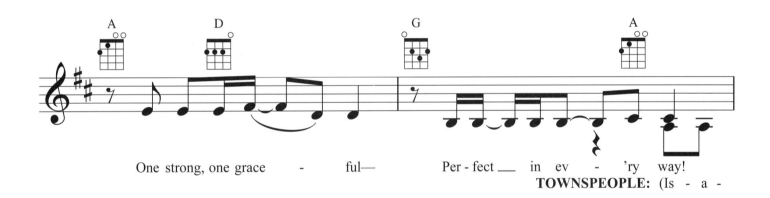

bel - la!) ___ Grows a flow - er, the town goes wild. ___ (Is - a -

bel - la!) ___ She's the per - fect gold - en

- ti - cal ___ and mag - i - cal. ___ That's who we are in the Fam - ily...

Mad - ri - gal! *(Spoken:) ¡Adios! Ooo!* **TOWN KID:** *But what's your gift?* Ha!

Chorus

Well, I ___ got - ta go, the life ___ of a Mad - ri - gal! (Whoa) ___

But now ___ you all know the Fam - i - ly Mad - ri - gal! (Whoa) ___

I nev - er meant ___ this to ___ get au - to - bi - o - graph - i - cal, ___

So just ___ to re - view, the Fam - i - ly Mad - ri - gal, let's go...

TOWN KIDS: (But what a - bout

Outro

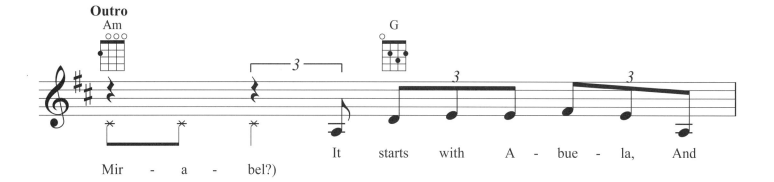

Mir - a - bel?)

It starts with A - bue - la, And

then *tí - a* Pe - pa, she han - dles the weath - er...

(But what a - bout

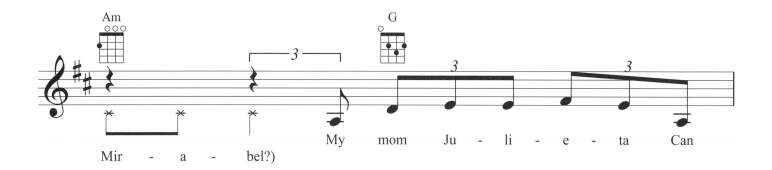

Mir - a - bel?)

My mom Ju - li - e - ta Can

make you feel bet - ter with just one *a - re - pa.*

(But what a - bout

My dad Ag-us-tín,   well, He's ac-ci-dent prone but he means   well.
Mir - a - bel?)   (But   what a-bout

Hey you said you wan-na know what   Ev-'ry-one does, I   got sis-ters and cous-ins and...
Mir - a - bel?)

My *pri - mo* Ca - mi - lo won't stop un - til   he makes you smile   to - day!

TOWN KIDS:
(Mir - a - bel!)

My cous - in Do - lo - res can   hear this whole cho - rus   a   mile   a - way!

TOWN KIDS:
(Mir - a - bel!)

Look!   It's Mis   -   ter   Mar - i - a - no,   hey

TOWN KIDS:
(Mir - a - bel!)

You can mar - ry my sis - ter if you wan - na Be -

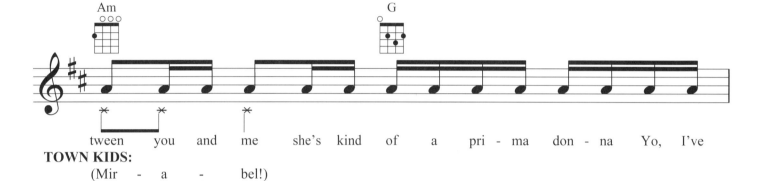

tween you and me she's kind of a pri - ma don - na Yo, I've

TOWN KIDS:
(Mir - a - bel!)

said too much and thank __ you but I real - ly got - ta

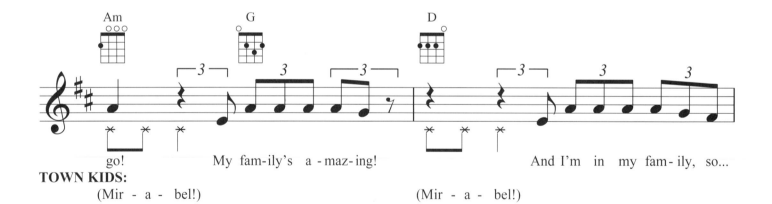

go! My fam-ily's a - maz-ing! And I'm in my fam-ily, so...

TOWN KIDS:
(Mir - a - bel!) (Mir - a - bel!)

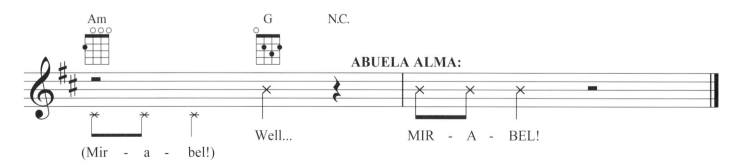

ABUELA ALMA:

(Mir - a - bel!) Well... MIR - A - BEL!

Waiting on a Miracle

Music and Lyrics by Lin-Manuel Miranda

* Vocal sung one octave lower than written.

Chorus

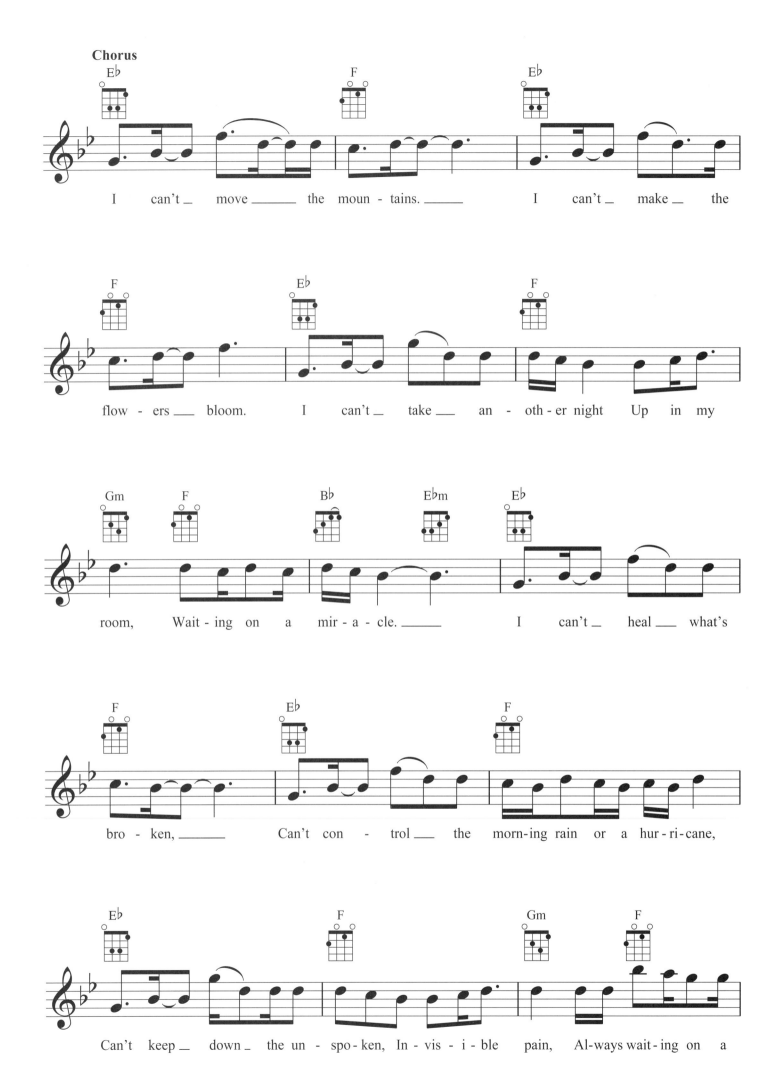

Bridge

mir - a - cle, a mir - a - cle... Al - ways walk - ing a - lone, _____

Al - ways want - ing ___ for more, _____ Like I'm still at that

door _____ Long - ing to shine ___ like all of you shine. _____

All I need is a change, _____ All I need is a

chance, _____ All I know is I can't ___ stay on the side. _

Chorus

16

Outro

_____ some-thing new, Who I ____ am ____ in - side. ____ So what can I

do? I'm sick of wait-ing on a mir-a-cle, So here I go... I am read-y! ____

C-'mon, I'm ____ read-y! ____ I've been pa - tient and stead-fast and stead-y! ____

Bless me now ____ as you blessed us All those years a - go, When you gave us a

Slowly, freely

mir-a-cle. ____ Am I too late for a mir-a-cle?

Surface Pressure

Music and Lyrics by Lin-Manuel Miranda

Vocal sung one octave lower than written.

whoa _ oh oh. ___ Give it to your sis - ter, your sis-ter's strong — er,

See if she can hang on a lit - tle long — er. Who _

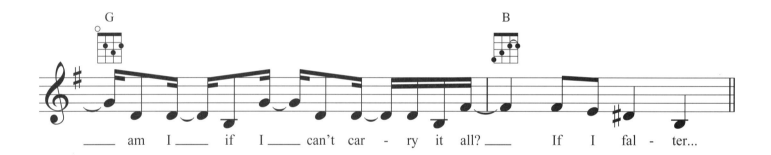

___ am I ___ if I ___ can't car - ry it all? ___ If I fal - ter...

Verse
Straight 16ths

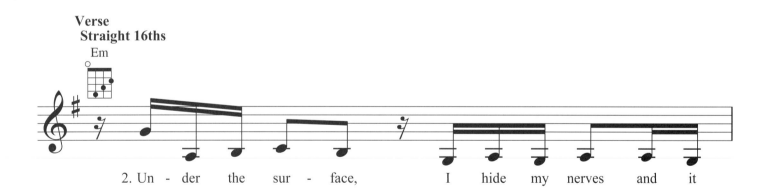

2. Un - der the sur - face, I hide my nerves and it

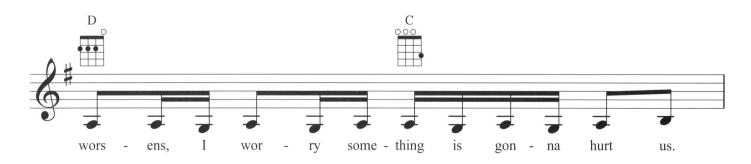

wors - ens, I wor - ry some - thing is gon - na hurt us.

Un - der   the   sur - face,   The   ship   does - n't

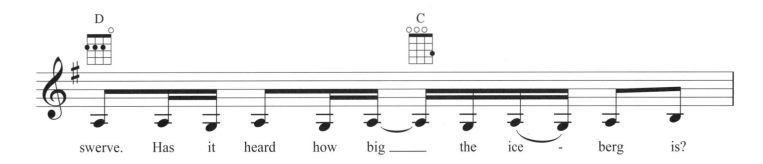

swerve. Has   it   heard   how   big _____ the   ice - berg   is?

Swing 16ths

Un - der   the   sur - face,   I   think   a - bout   my

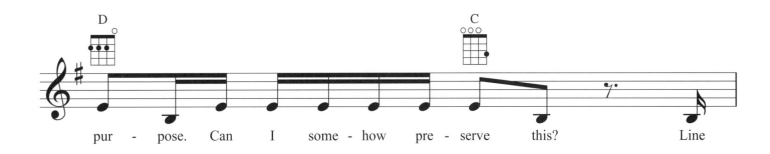

pur - pose. Can   I   some - how   pre - serve   this?   Line

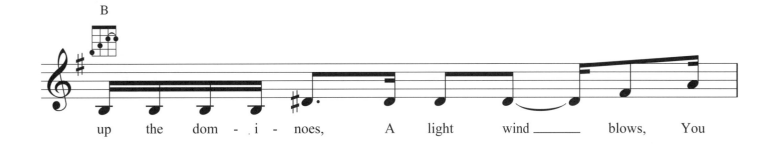

up   the   dom - i - noes,   A   light   wind _____ blows,   You

try   to   stop   it   top - pl - in'   but   on   and   on   it   goes.   But

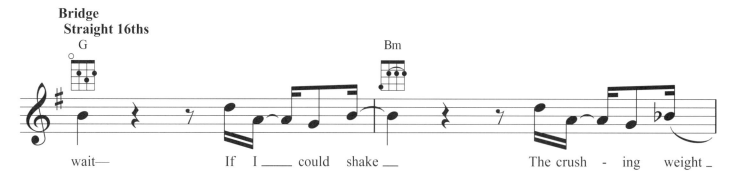

Bridge
Straight 16ths

wait— If I ___ could shake ___ The crush - ing weight ___

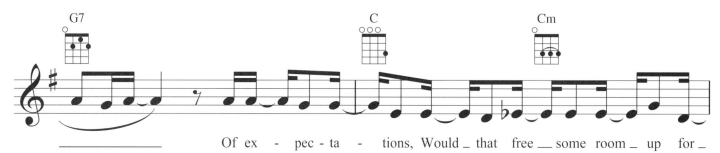

_____ Of ex - pec - ta - tions, Would _ that free _ some room _ up for _

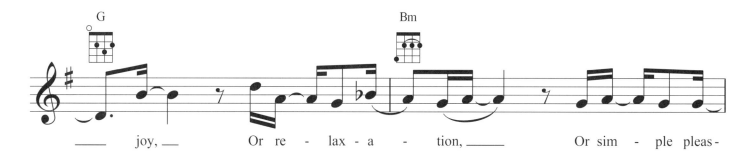

___ joy, ___ Or re - lax - a - tion, _____ Or sim - ple pleas -

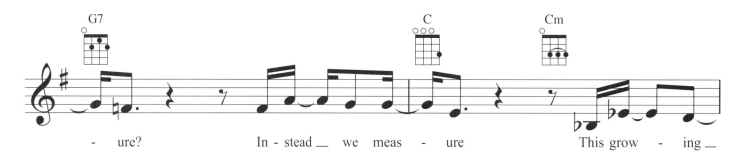

- ure? In - stead _ we meas - ure This grow - ing _

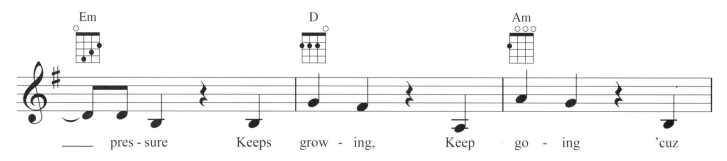

_____ pres - sure Keeps grow - ing, Keep go - ing 'cuz

D.S. al Coda
(Back to Swing 16ths)

all we know is...

Coda

_____

Chorus

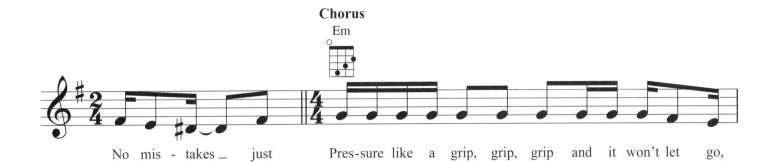

No mis - takes _ just Pres-sure like a grip, grip, grip and it won't let go,

whoa. _ Pres-sure like a tick, tick, tick 'til it's read - y to blow, _

_____ whoa _ oh oh. ___ Give it to your sis - ter, and nev-er won - der If __

_____ the same pres - sure would - 've pulled you un - der. Who _

_____ am I ___ if I ___ don't have _ what it takes? _ No cracks, no...

breaks, No mis - takes! _ No pres - sure!

We Don't Talk About Bruno

Music and Lyrics by Lin-Manuel Miranda

Verse

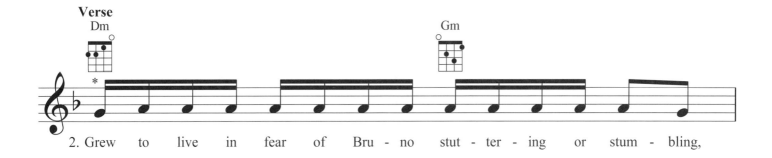

2. Grew to live in fear of Bru - no stut - ter - ing or stum - bling,

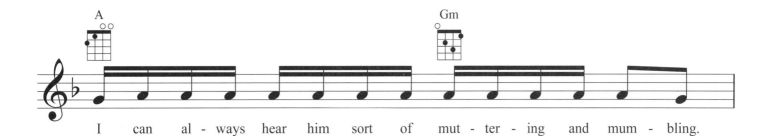

I can al - ways hear him sort of mut - ter - ing and mum - bling.

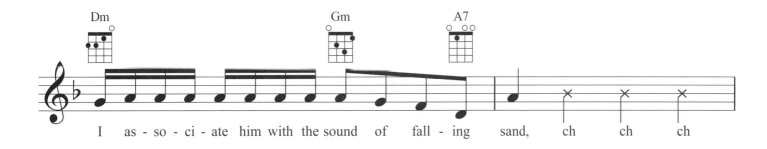

I as - so - ci - ate him with the sound of fall - ing sand, ch ch ch

It's a heav - y lift, with a gift so hum - bling,

Al - ways left A - bue - la and the fam - i - ly fum - bling,

Grap - pl - ing with proph - e - cies they could - n't un - der -

* Vocal sung an octave lower than written.

Chorus

CAMILO:

stand. Do you un - der - stand? A sev - en - foot frame, Rats

a - long his back, When he calls your name It all

fades to black. Yeah, he sees your dreams, And feasts

PEPA, FÉLIX
CAMILO & DOLORES:

on your screams We don't talk a - bout Bru -

- no, no, no, no! We don't talk a - bout Bru -

Verse

TOWNSWOMAN WITH FISH:

- no! 3. He told me my fish would die. The next

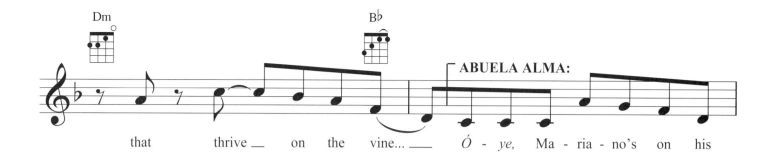

that   thrive __ on the vine... __ Ó - *ye,* Ma - ria - no's on his

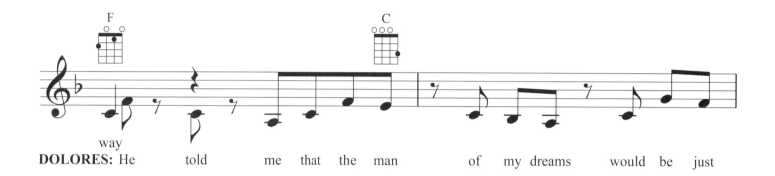

way
DOLORES: He   told   me that the man   of my dreams   would be just

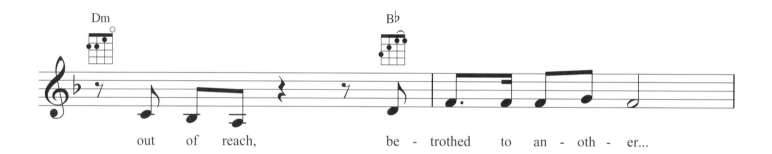

out   of reach,   be - trothed   to an - oth - er...

It's   like   I   hear   him ___ now. ___

ISABELA:

Hey   sis, ___   I want

It's like I can hear him now, ___ I can hear him now!

not a sound ___ out of you... ___

Interlude

MIRABEL:

Um, Bru - no... Yeah, a - bout that Bru - no... I

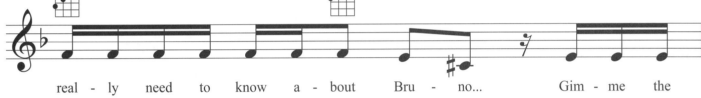

real - ly need to know a - bout Bru - no... Gim - me the

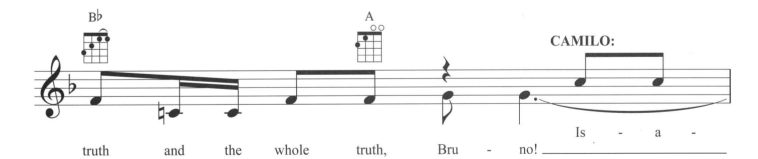

CAMILO:

truth and the whole truth, Bru - no! ___ Is - a -

JULIETA & PEPA: **CAMILO:**

bel - a, your boy - friend's here.   Time for din - ner!   A

Chorus

sev - en - foot frame, Rats _____ a - long his back, When he

calls your _____ name It all _____ fades _____ to black. Yeah, he

sees your _____ dreams, And feasts _____ on _____ your screams

PEPA:

You tell - ing this sto - ry or _____ am I?

Outro-Chorus

ABUELA ALMA: CAMILO:

Ó - ye, Ma - ria - no's on his way   A sev - en - foot frame, Rats _

_____ a - long his back. When he calls your _____ name it all _____

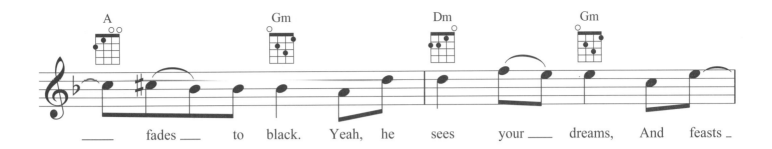

_ fades _ to black. Yeah, he sees your _ dreams, And feasts _

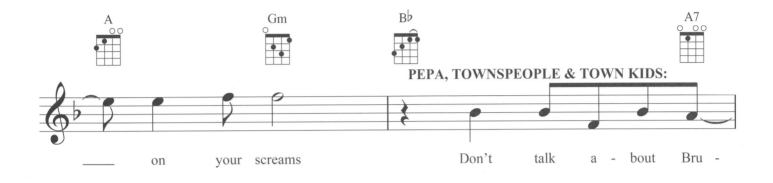

PEPA, TOWNSPEOPLE & TOWN KIDS:

_ on your screams   Don't talk a - bout Bru -

- no, _ no! _   Not a word a - bout Bru -

MIRABEL:

Why did I talk a - bout Bru - no?!   I

- no! _____

nev - er should - a brought up Bru - no!

What Else Can I Do?

Music and Lyrics by Lin-Manuel Miranda

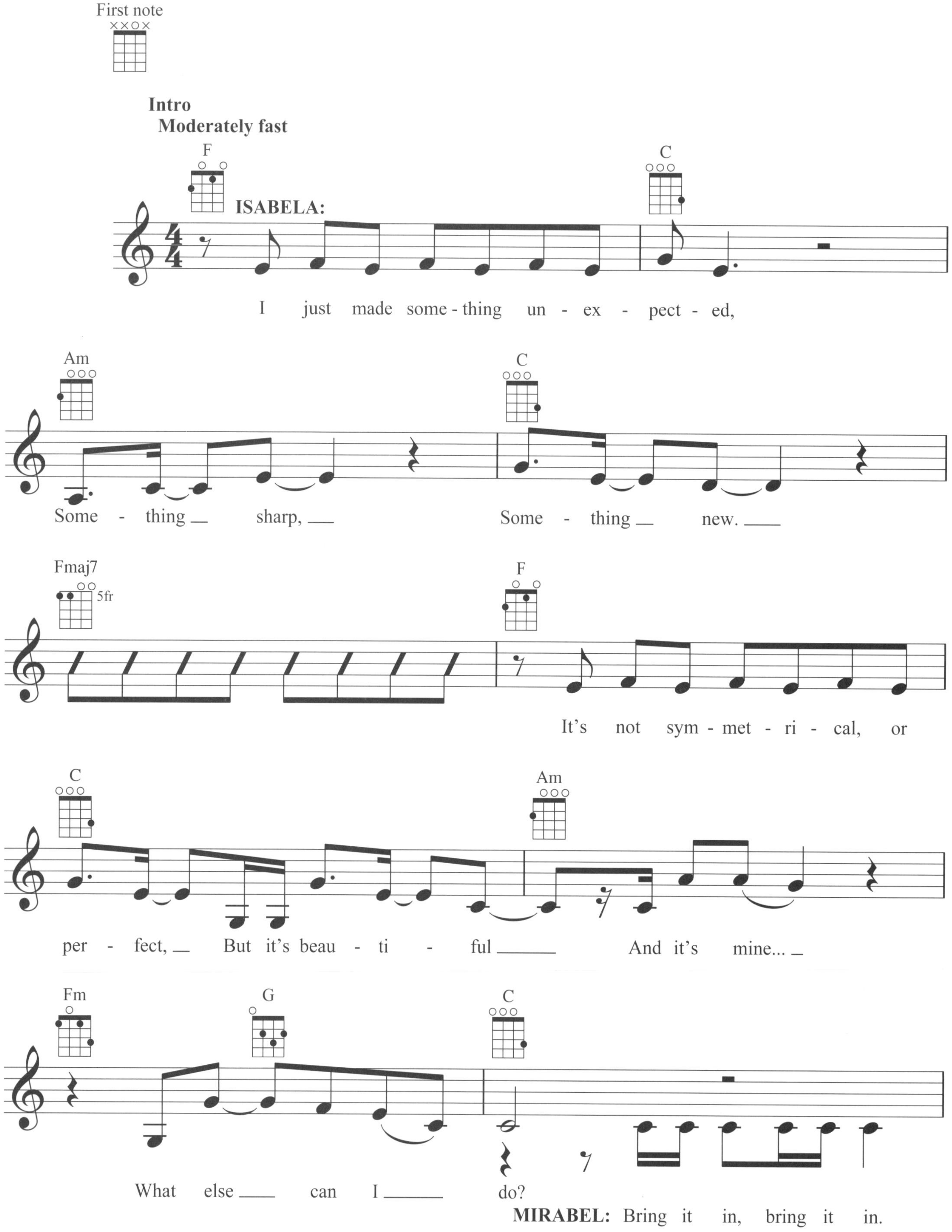

First note
Intro
Moderately fast
F
C
ISABELA:
I just made some - thing un - ex - pect - ed,
Am
C
Some - thing sharp, Some - thing new.
Fmaj7
5fr
F
It's not sym - met - ri - cal, or
C
Am
per - fect, But it's beau - ti - ful And it's mine...
Fm
G
C
What else can I do?
MIRABEL: Bring it in, bring it in.

What else _____ can _ I _____ do? _____

Good talk, bring it in, bring it in. Let's walk, bring it in, bring it in.

Verse

ISABELA:

_____ Free hugs! bring it in, bring it in.

1. I grow rows _____ and rows

_____ of ros - es. *Flor de may - o,*

By the mile. _____ I make per - fect, prac -

- ticed pos - es. So much hides _____ be - hind _____

Pre-Chorus

_____ my smile. _____ What could I do if I just

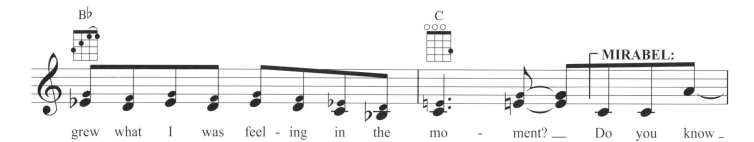

grew what I was feel-ing in the mo - ment? __ Do you know __

ISABELA:

__ where you're go - ing? Whoa... What could I do if I just

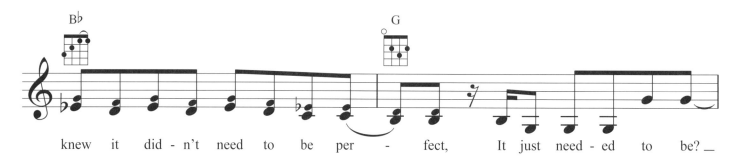

knew it did-n't need to be per - fect, It just need-ed to be? __

Chorus

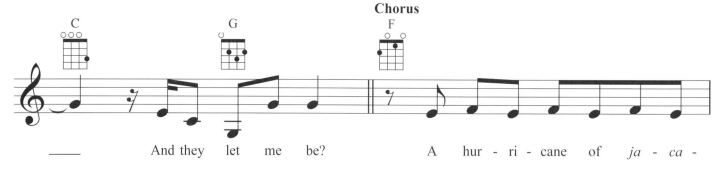

__ And they let me be? A hur - ri - cane of *ja - ca -*

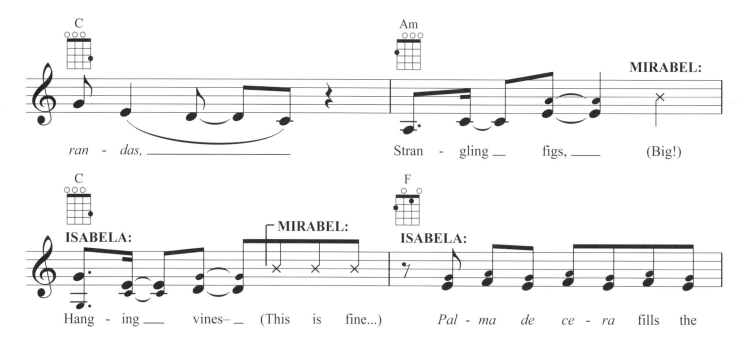

MIRABEL:

ran - das, __ Stran - gling __ figs, __ (Big!)

ISABELA: **MIRABEL:** **ISABELA:**

Hang - ing __ vines– __ (This is fine...) *Pal - ma de ce - ra* fills the

air as I _____ climb ____ And I ____ push through... _

Bridge 1

____ What else ____ can I ____ do? ____ Can I de-

liv - er us a riv - er of sun - dew? _____ Care - ful it's car-

niv - o - rous, a lit - tle just won't do... ____ I wan - na feel the

shiv - er of some - thing new. _____ I'm so sick of

Bridge 2

pret - ty, I want some-thing true, don't you? **MIRABEL:** You just seem Like your life's

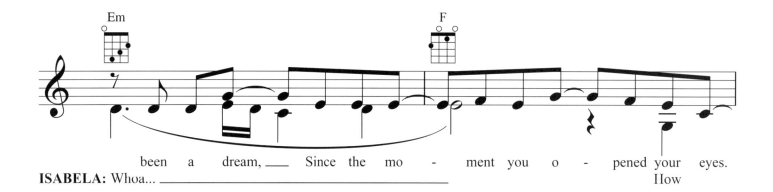

been a dream, ___ Since the mo - ment you o - pened your eyes.
ISABELA: Whoa... _____ How

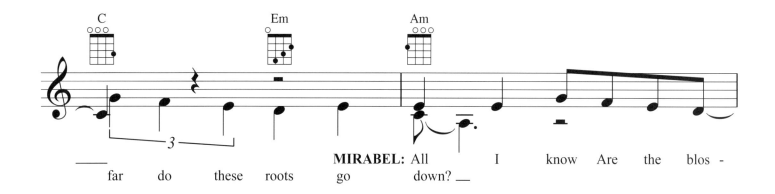

___ far do these roots go down? _
MIRABEL: All I know Are the blos -

\- soms you grow, But it's awe - some to see ___ how you rise. _
Whoa... _____

BOTH:
___ How far ___ can you rise? ___ Through the roof, to the skies _
How far ___ can I rise? ___ Through the roof, to the skies _

Chorus

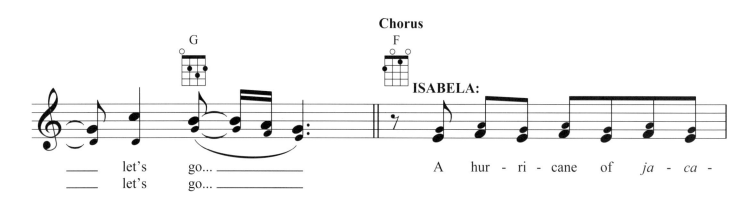

ISABELA:
___ let's go... _____ A hur - ri - cane of *ja - ca -*
___ let's go... _____

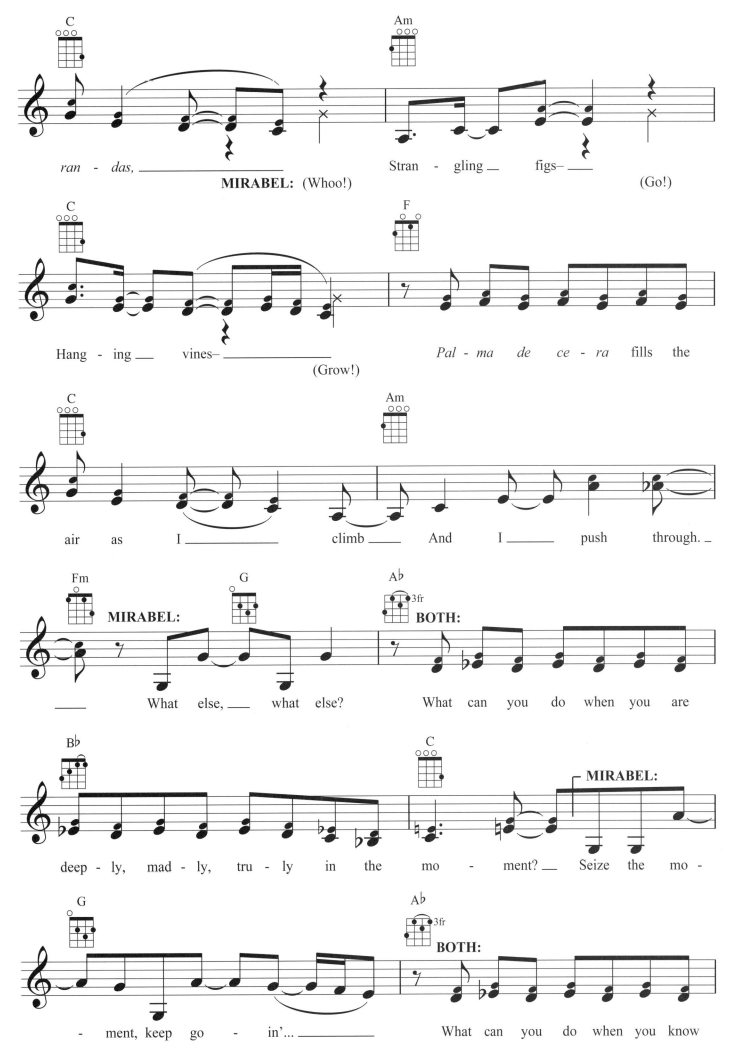

here, and well, ___ I owe ___ this all ___ to you. ___

Outro

___ What else ___ can I ___ do? ___

Show 'em what you can do— ___

What else ___ can I ___ do? ___

There's noth - ing you can't do— ___

What else ___ can I do? ___

Dos Oruguitas

Music and Lyrics by Lin-Manuel Miranda

Interlude

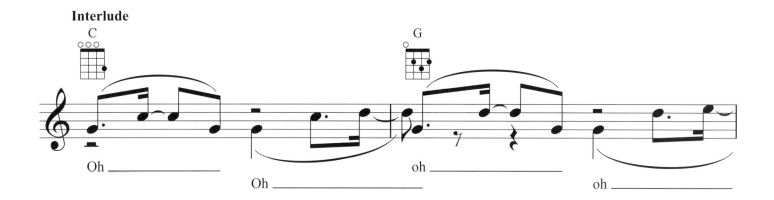

Oh _____
Oh _____   oh _____   oh _____

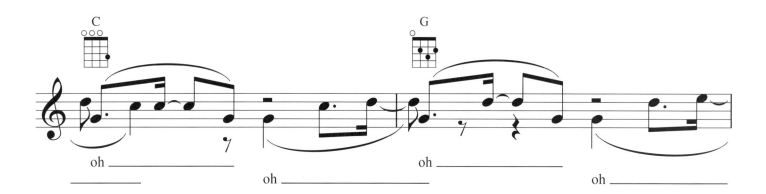

oh _____   oh _____   oh _____   oh _____
_____   oh _____

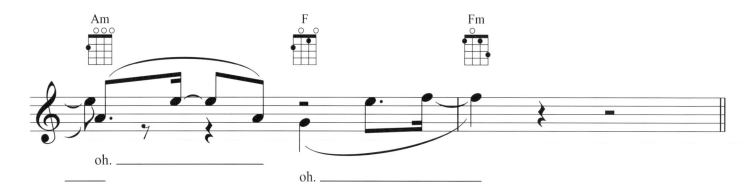

oh _____   oh _____   oh _____   oh _____
_____   oh _____

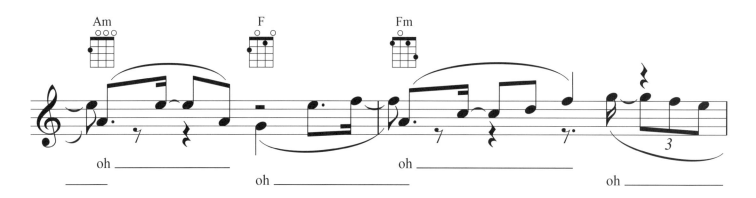

oh. _____
_____   oh. _____

Verse

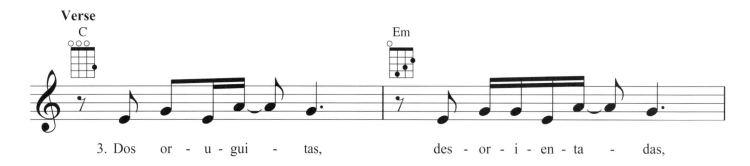

3. Dos or - u - gui - tas,   des - or - i - en - ta - das,

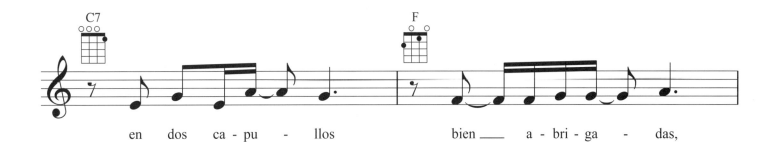

en dos ca-pu-llos bien ___ a-bri-ga - das,

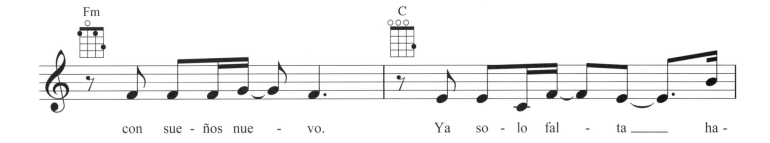

con sue-ños nue - vo. Ya so-lo fal - ta ___ ha-

cer lo ne - ce-sa - rio en el mun - do qu si - gue cam-bian-do. Tum-

ban-do sus ___ pa-re - des, ah-i vie - ne nues - tro mi-

la-gro... (nues - tro mi-la-gro...) oh. ___
(nues - tro mi-la-gro...) (nues - tro mi-la-gro...)

Lead vocal melody 2nd/3rd time.
**Lead vocal melody 3rd time.*

All of You

Music and Lyrics by Lin-Manuel Miranda

First note

Verse
Gently

1. Look at ___ this home, ___ We need a new ___ foun - da - tion.

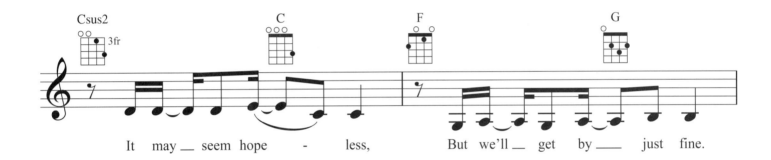

It may ___ seem hope - less, But we'll ___ get by ___ just fine.

Look at ___ this fam - ily, A glow-ing con - stel - la - tion

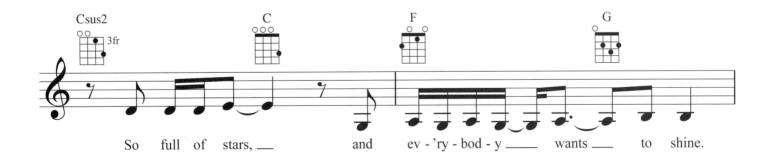

So full of stars, ___ and ev - 'ry-bod - y ___ wants ___ to shine.

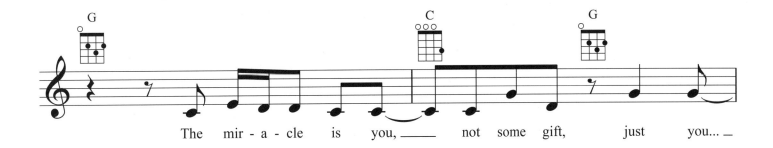

The mir-a-cle is you, ____ not some gift, just you... ____

add JULIETA, PEPA:

____ The mir-a-cle is you. ____ All of you, ____ all of you. ____

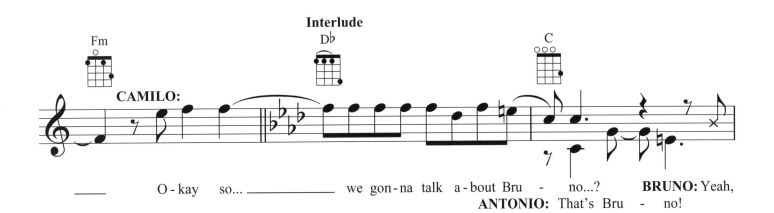

Interlude

CAMILO:

____ O-kay so... ____ we gon-na talk a-bout Bru - no...? **BRUNO:** Yeah,

ANTONIO: That's Bru - no!

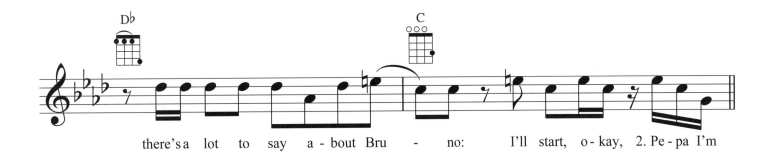

there's a lot to say a-bout Bru - no: I'll start, o-kay, 2. Pe-pa I'm

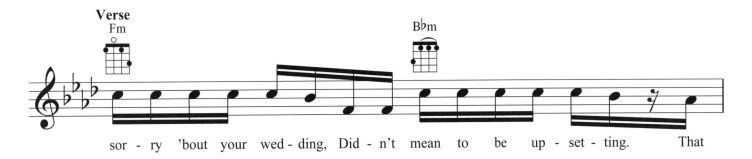

Verse

sor-ry 'bout your wed-ding, Did-n't mean to be up-set-ting. That

was-n't a proph-e-cy I could just see you were sweat-ing! And I

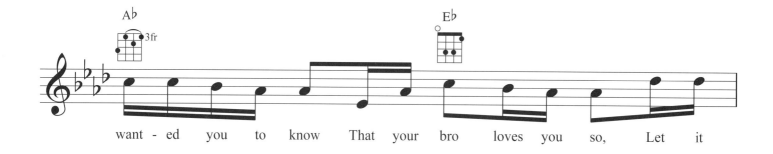

want-ed you to know That your bro loves you so, Let it

in, let it out, let it rain, let it snow, "Let it gooo..." _

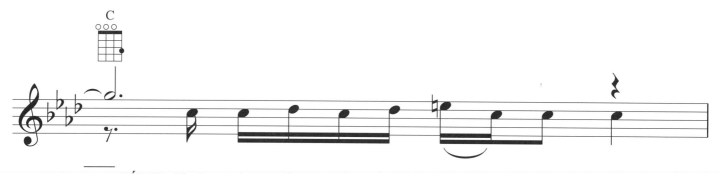

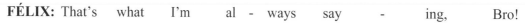

FÉLIX: That's what I'm al - ways say - ing, Bro!

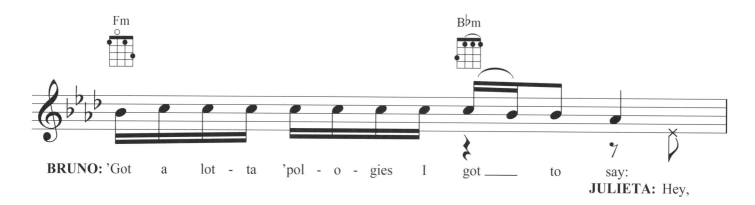

BRUNO: 'Got a lot - ta 'pol - o - gies I got _____ to say:

JULIETA: Hey,

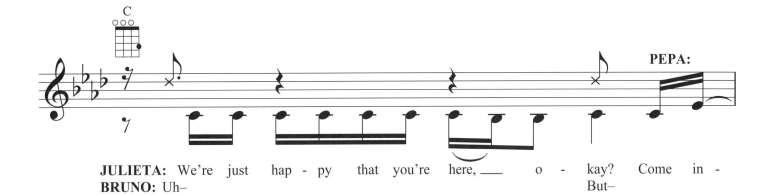

JULIETA: We're just hap - py that you're here, ___ o - kay? Come in -
BRUNO: Uh–

\- to the light! The trip - lets all re - u - nite! And no
But–

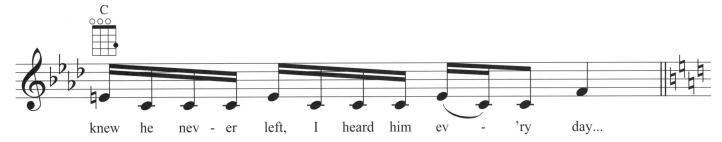

mat - ter what hap - pens We're gon - na find ___ our ___ way.

Yo I

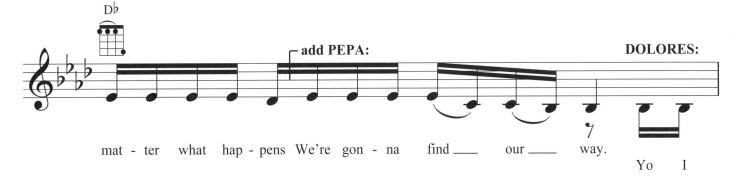

knew he nev - er left, I heard him ev - 'ry day...

Interlude

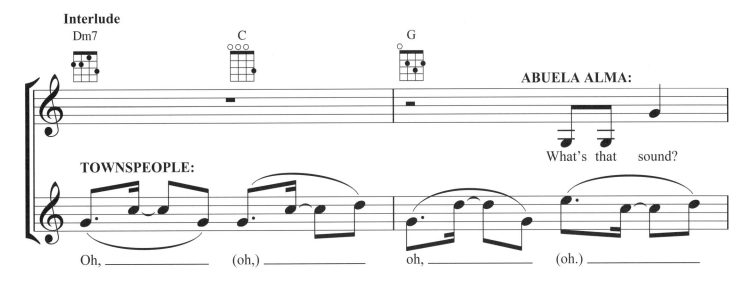

ABUELA ALMA:

What's that sound?

TOWNSPEOPLE:

Oh, _____ (oh,) _____ oh, _____ (oh.)

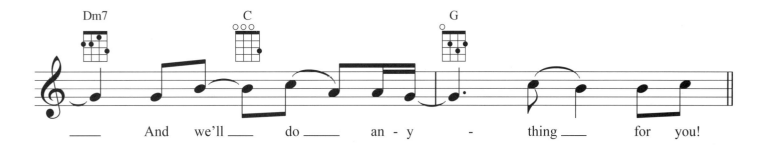

And we'll do an - y - thing for you!

Verse

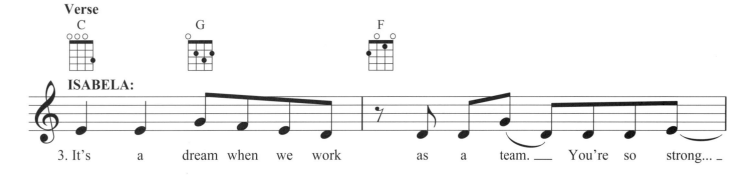

ISABELA:

3. It's a dream when we work as a team. You're so strong...

LUISA:
MIRABEL:
ISABELA:
LUISA:

Yeah, but some - times I cry– So do I! I

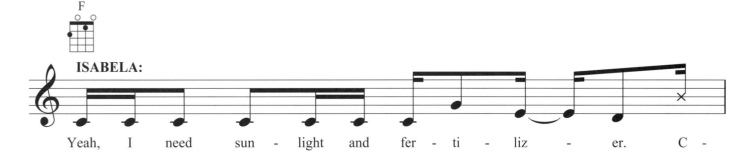

may not be as strong, but I'm get - ting wis - er.

ISABELA:

Yeah, I need sun - light and fer - ti - liz - er. C -

'mon! Let's plant some - thing new and watch it fly,

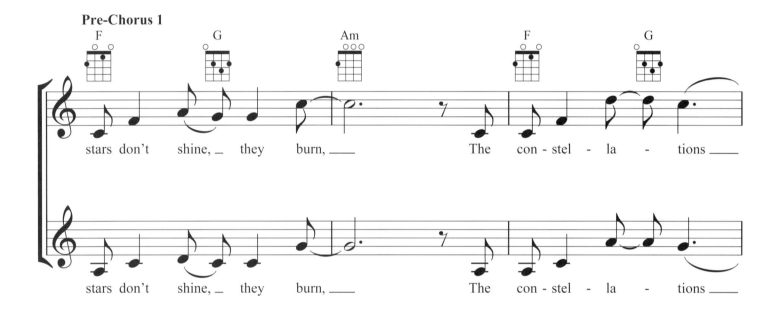

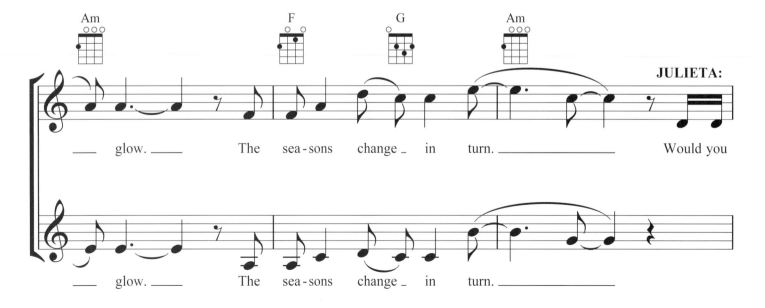

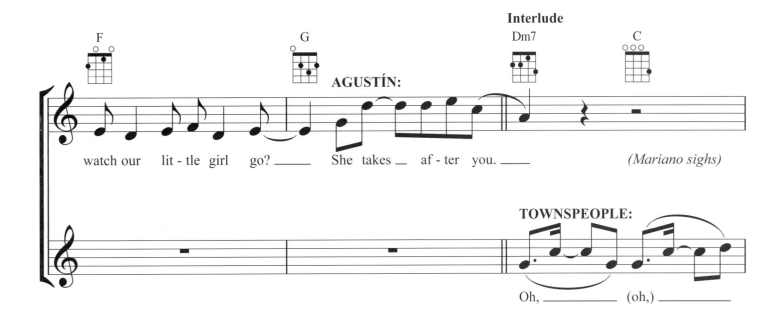

seiz - ing the mo - ment, so would you wake up and no - tice me? ___

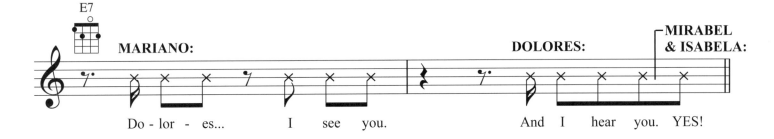

MARIANO: Do - lor - es... I see you. **DOLORES:** And I hear you. **MIRABEL & ISABELA:** YES!

Interlude

TOWNSPEOPLE: All of you, ___ all of you. ___ **MARIANO:** Let's get mar - ried! **DOLORES:** Slow down.

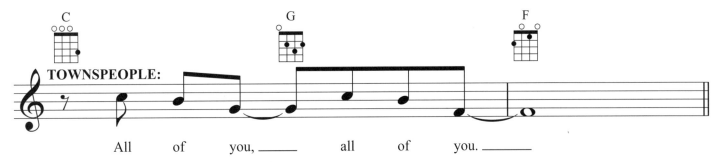

TOWNSPEOPLE: All of you, ___ all of you. ___

Verse

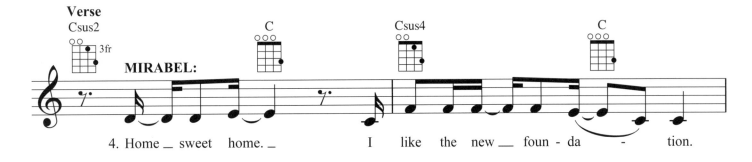

MIRABEL: 4. Home ___ sweet home. ___ I like the new ___ foun - da - tion.

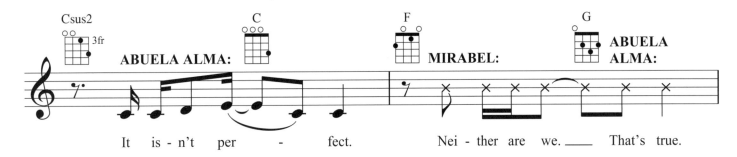

ABUELA ALMA: It is - n't per - fect. **MIRABEL:** Nei - ther are we. ___ **ABUELA ALMA:** That's true.

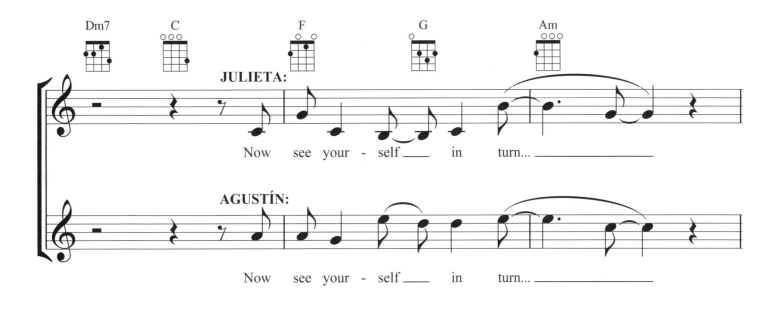

JULIETA: Now see your - self ___ in turn... ___

AGUSTÍN: Now see your - self ___ in turn... ___

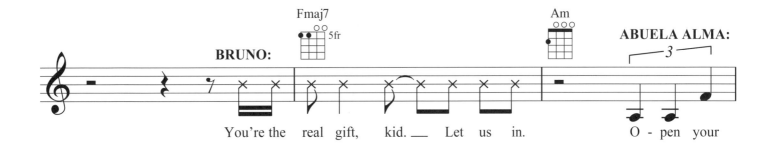

BRUNO: You're the real gift, kid. __ Let us in.

ABUELA ALMA: O - pen your

Outro
Slower

ABUELA ALMA:

eyes. *Abre los ojos.* *What do you see?*

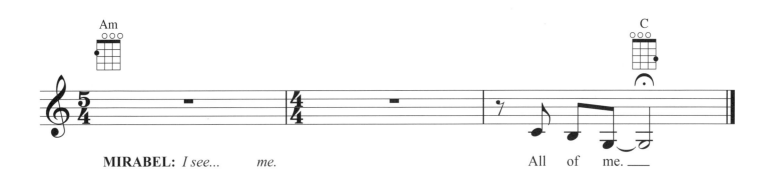

MIRABEL: *I see... me.* All of me. ___

Colombia, Mi Encanto

Music and Lyrics by Lin-Manuel Miranda

Mi - la - gros en ca - da pi - so.

(A - e, a - e, a - e, a - e, a -

En - can - to   En - can - to

e,   a - e,   a - e.)

𝄋 **Chorus**

Co - lom - bia, te qui - e - ro tan - to _____

Que siem - pre me en - a - mo - ra tu en - can - to. ___

Co - lom - bia, te qui - e - ro tan - to _____

{ Que si - gas ben - di - cien - do tu en - can - to... __ }
{ Te si - gue ben - di - cien - do tu en - can - to... __ }   Co -

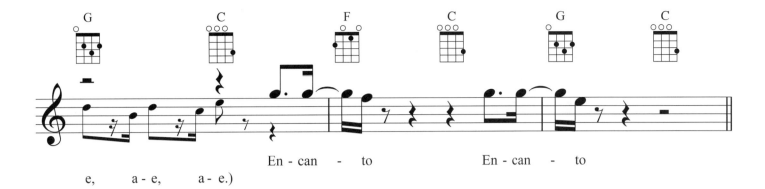

En - can - to   En - can - to

e,   a - e,   a - e.)

Bridge

N.C.

Co - lom - bia, te a - do - ro tan - to.   Tu nom - bre tie - ne un en - can - to.

De Bo - go - tá has - ta Pa - len - que   Me fui _ con to - da la gen - te.

Co - lom - bia, tie - rra tan be - lla,   La ma - dre na - tu - ra - le - za

Te dio un - a for - ma de ser. *Co - lom - bi - a stays, _ my fa - vor - ite place. _*

Chorus

Co - lom - bia, te qui - er - o tan - to _____
Y es que a ti Co - lom - bia yo te qui - er - o tan - to _____

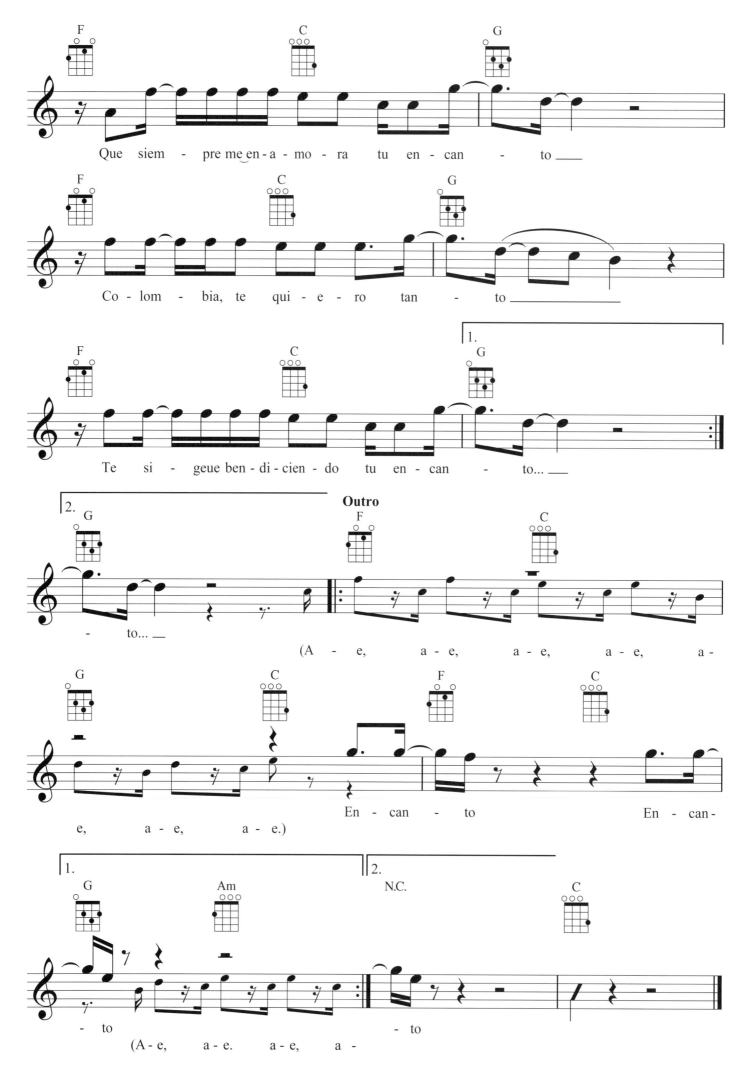

Que siem - pre me en-a - mo - ra tu en - can - to ____

Co - lom - bia, te qui - e - ro tan - to _____

1.

Te si - gue ben - di - cien - do tu en - can - to... __

2.   **Outro**

- to... __

(A - e,   a - e,   a - e,   a - e,   a -

En - can - to   En - can -

e,   a - e,   a - e.)

1.   2.

- to   - to

(A - e,   a - e.   a - e,   a -

Two Oruguitas

Music and Lyrics by Lin-Manuel Miranda

1. Two *or - u - gui - tas* In love and yearn - ing,
2. Two *or - u - gui - tas* A - gainst the weath - er.

Spend ev - 'ry eve - ning and morn - ing learn - ing
The wind grows cold - er, But they're to - geth - er.

To hold each oth - er, Their hun - ger burn - ing ___ To
They hold each oth - er, No way of know - ing ___ They're

nav - i - gate a world ___ That turns ___ and nev - er stops turn - ing. To-
all they have for shel - ter, And some - thing in - side ___ them is grow - ing. They

geth - er in this world ___ That turns ___ and nev - er stops turn - ing.
long to stay to - geth - er, But some-

Interlude

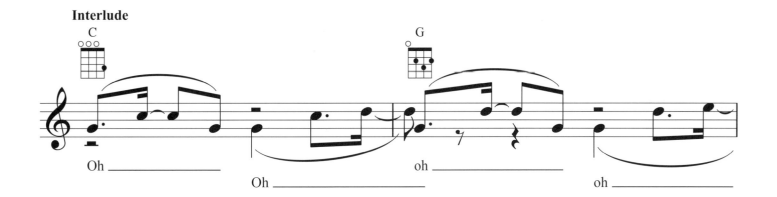

Oh _____ oh _____ oh _____

Oh _____ oh _____

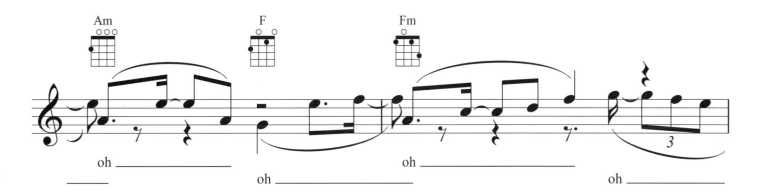

oh _____ oh _____ oh _____

oh _____

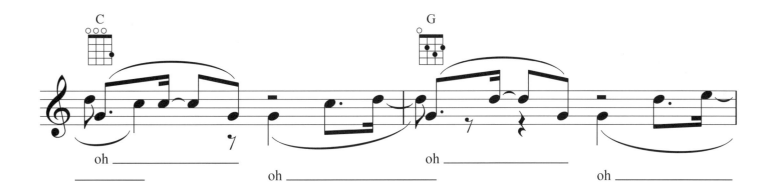

oh _____ oh _____ oh _____

oh _____

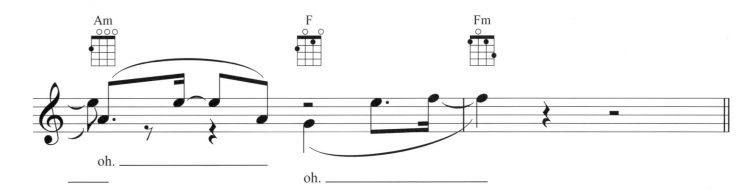

oh. _____

oh. _____

Verse

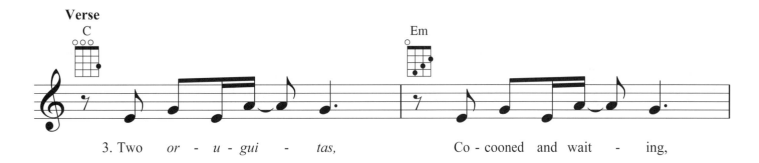

3. Two *or - u - gui - tas,* Co - cooned and wait - ing,

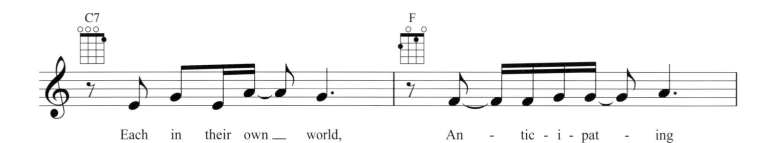

Each in their own __ world,   An - tic - i - pat - ing

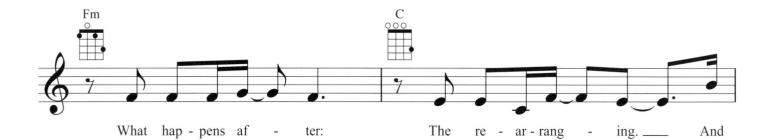

What hap - pens af - ter: The re - ar - rang - ing. __   And

so a - fraid __ of change, __   In a world __ that nev - er stops chang - ing.   So

let the walls __ come down, __   The world ____ will nev - er stop

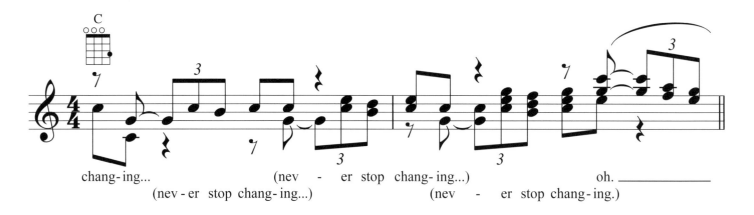

chang - ing...   (nev - er stop chang - ing...)   oh. _____
(nev - er stop chang - ing...)   (nev - er stop chang - ing.)

Chorus

Ay, ___ mar - i - po - sas, ___ don't ___ you hold on too tight.

Both ___ of you know It's your time to go, to fly a - part, to re - u - nite.

Won - ders sur - round you, ___ Just ___ let the walls come down.

Don't look be - hind you, Fly ___ 'til you find Your way toward to - mor - row. ___

find Your way toward to - mor - row. ___

* Lead vocal melody 2nd/3rd time.
** Lead vocal melody 3rd time.